CHRISTMAS
FACTS, FIGURES
& FUN

CAMERON BROWN

"Any book without a mistake in it has had too much money spent on it"

Sir William Collins, publisher

CHRISTMAS
Facts, Figures & Fun

Cameron Brown

ff&f

Christmas
Facts, Figures & Fun

Published by
Facts, Figures & Fun, an imprint of
AAPPL Artists' and Photographers' Press Ltd.
10 Hillside, London SW19 4NH, UK
info@ffnf.co.uk   www.ffnf.co.uk
info@aappl.com   www.aappl.com

Sales and Distribution
UK and export: Turnaround Publisher Services Ltd.
orders@turnaround-uk.com
USA and Canada: Sterling Publishing Inc. sales@sterlingpub.com
Australia & New Zealand: Peribo Pty. peribomec@bigpond.com
South Africa: Trinity Books. trinity@iafrica.com

A catalogue record for this book is available from the
British Library.

ISBN 1-904332-27-7

Design (contents and cover): Malcolm Couch
mal.couch@blueyonder.co.uk

Printed in China by Imago Publishing
info@imago.co.uk

CONTENTS

CHRISTMAS, AN INTRODUCTION

At Christmas play and make good cheer,
For Christmas comes but once a year.
Thomas Tusser "The Farmer's Daily Diet"

The word *Christmas* is a contraction of *Christ's Mass*, derived from the Old English *Cristes mæsse*. *Christ* comes from the Greek word *christos* meaning the a*nointed* or *consecrated one* - the title given to Jesus. *Christos* is the word generally used as the translation of the Hebrew *mashiah* (our word *messiah*).

Christians first started celebrating the birth of Jesus around 400 AD. At this time there was no established tradition of December 25 as Jesus' birthday but mid-December was the time of many pagan festivals. Early scholars and churchmen disputed the exact date for centuries as it is not given anywhere in the bible. It settled on the present date some time in the 4th Century but, because of the change from the Julian to the Gregorian calendar in 1752 this date is not accepted by some people, who still celebrate Christ's birth on January 7, the day which would have been December 25 had the calendar not been changed.

In predominantly Christian countries, Christmas has become the most economically important holiday of the year, characterized by the giving of gifts within families, and between friends and by gifts brought by Santa Claus or other mythical figures. Local and regional Christmas traditions differ greatly despite the widespread influence of American and British Christmas, motifs through literature, television, and other mass media. Christmas is also celebrated as a secular holiday in many countries with small Christian populations.

Christmas is often abbreviated to *Xmas*, because the letter X resembles the Greek letter *Chi,* which is the first letter of *Christ* as spelled in Greek. This was originally an ecclesiastical abbreviation but in the early days of printing, when font sizes were limited and type was set by hand, abbreviations were used liberally and Xmas came into general and perfectly acceptable popular use.

"Christmas is a time when everybody wants his past forgotten and his present remembered."
Anon

Christmas is …

"Christmas is not a time nor a season, but a state of mind. To cherish peace and goodwill, to be plenteous in mercy, is to have the real spirit of Christmas."
Calvin Coolidge

"Christmas is the one time of year when people of all religions come together to worship Jesus Christ."
Bart Simpson

"Christmas… is not an eternal event at all, but a piece of one's home that one carries in one's heart…"
Freya Stark

"Christmas is the Disneyfication of Christianity"
Don Cupitt

"Christmas is a time when you get homesick – even when you're home."
Carol Nelson

"Christmas is the time when kids tell Santa what they want and adults pay for it. Deficits are when adults tell government what they want and their kids pay for it."
Richard Lamm

"Christmas is coming, the geese are getting fat,
Please to put a penny in an old man's hat;
If you haven't got a penny a ha'penny will do,
If you haven't got a ha'penny, God bless you."
Mother Goose

Adoration of the Magi
11th century

THE CHRISTMAS STORY

----------- THE GOSPEL STORIES -----------

The story of Christ's birth is dealt with in the bible in the gospels of Matthew and Luke; Mark and John do not mention Jesus' childhood, and those of Matthew and Luke give differing accounts, Luke's being closest to the modern idea of the Christmas story and his is the version most often read in Christmas church services.

In Luke's gospel, Mary learns from an angel that she will have a child created in her body by the Holy Ghost, resulting in the so-called *virgin birth*. Shortly thereafter, she and her husband Joseph leave their home in Nazareth to register for the Roman census in the town of Bethlehem. Unable to get accomodation in any of the inns in the town, all of which are full, they are obliged to shelter in a stable, where Mary gives birth to Jesus in a manger, (a feeding trough or stall). Christ's birth in Bethlehem of Judea, the home of the house of David from which Joseph was descended, fulfilled the prophecy of Isaiah about the coming of the saviour, or Messiah.

Matthew's gospel also mentions the virgin birth of Jesus but then moves directly to the coming of the wise men from the East to the home where Christ was staying after his birth in Bethlehem. The wise men (*magi*), first went to Jerusalem to tell King Herod that they had seen a star signalling the birth of the king of the Jews. Herod sent them to find this king so that he himself could go and worship him. The star then led them to Bethlehem and the home of Mary and Joseph. They presented Jesus with treasures of gold, frankincense, and myrrh. The wise men or three kings left without telling Herod of their succesful quest as each of them had dreamed that Herod would try to kill the child to protect his own position as ruler. The gospel then goes on to relate how Herod ordered the killing of all the children in Bethlehem aged 2 or less, but that Mary and her family, also warned by God in a dream, had escaped by fleeing to Egypt, returning only after Herod's death to live in Nazareth.

In Bethlehem, the town where Jesus is said to have been born, in modern-day Israel, is the site of the Church of the Nativity. On December 24 each year visitors crowd the church's doorways and stand on the roof to watch the dramatic annual procession. Galloping horsemen and mounted police lead a parade, followed by a horseman on a black horse carrying a cross. Then come the churchmen and government officials and the procession solemnly enters the doors and places an ancient effigy of the baby Jesus in the Church. The birthplace of Jesus is said to be marked in the grotto below the church.

"How many observe Christ's birthday! How few, his precepts!
O! 'tis easier to keep holidays than commandments."
Benjamin Franklin

THE THREE WISE MEN

The story of the magi has certainly passed from the gospels into popular tradition. Some Christmas carols refer to the shepherds observing a huge star directly over Bethlehem, and following it to the birthplace but the magi, who Matthew reports as seeing a giant star, have ususally been translated as *wise men* or as *kings*. They are said to have come from the East (Iran? Saudi Arabia?), with their gifts of gold, frankincense, and myrrh.

Magi is the plural of the Latin word *magus*; the Greek equivalent is *magoi*. This latter term is sometimes used in the context of *magician* though the Latin word came to be used to

signify *teacher* or *master* (as in *magistrate*). The *magi* were however also the dominant sacred caste of the *Medes*, and ancient Media, Persia, Assyria, and Babylonia had a magian priesthood at the time of the birth of Christ.

The gospels do not actually say that there were 3 magi but the number of gifts suggests that there were.

Supposing the magi came from Persia (Iran), the route to Jerusalem was a journey of between 1000 and 1200 miles and would have taken anything from three to twelve months by camel.

Gold was valued in biblical times, as now, as the most precious and noble of metals and was therefore a gift fit for a king or for a poor family. The king who brought the gold is popularly believed to have been Melchior.

The trade in frankincense *(boswellia thurifera)* was at its height during the days of the Roman Empire. It is a sweet smelling gum resin derived from the Boswellia tree which, at that time, grew in Arabia, India, and Ethiopia. Tradition says that it was presented to the baby Jesus by the black king, Balthasar. This resin is collected by cutting the bark of the trees and over a period of weeks it hardens into tear-drop shaped chunks which are broken off and can be powdered and made into ointments or perfumes. It was considered as valuable as gems or precious metals. The Romans burned frankincense on their altars and at cremations

Myrrh, an aromatic gum resin which also oozes from gashes cut in the bark of a small desert tree known as *commifora myrrha* or the *didin* tree, was an extremely valuable commodity during biblical times and was generally imported from Somaliland, India and Arabia. Caspar is credited as the king who brought the myrrh.

In some central and East European countries the initials CMB (Caspar, Melchior and Balthasar) are chalked over the front door of each house, together with the date of the new year (eg: CMB 2006), to welcome the three wise men.

The cathedral of Cologne in Germany contains what are claimed to be the remains of the magi; these, it is said, were discovered in Persia (Iran), brought to Constantinople (Istanbul) by St. Helena, transferred to Milan in the fifth century and to Cologne in 1163.

"We consider Christmas as the encounter,
the great encounter, the historical encounter,
the decisive encounter, between God and mankind.
He who has faith knows this truly;
let him rejoice."
Pope Paul VI

"Christmas gift suggestions: To your enemy, forgiveness.
To an opponent, tolerance. To a friend, your heart.
To a customer, service. To all, charity.
To every child, a good example. To yourself, respect."
Oren Arnold

THE RELIGIOUS CELEBRATION
OF CHRISTMAS

Christmas in England "began" in AD 596, when St Augustine arrived with his fellow monks to bring Christianity to the Anglo-Saxons.

The first Christmas observance in what is now the United States was celebrated in Spanish style by Hernando de Soto and his army, who set up their winter camp in the present day city of Tallahassee, Florida in 1539.

Neither scripture nor tradition has passed down a firm date for Christmas. In ancient Judaism, there was a common belief, which the early Christians inherited, that the prophets of Israel died on the same date as their conception. According to ancient western calculations, Jesus was crucified on March 25, so there was a presumption that March 25 was also the date of Jesus' conception. The *Annunciation* is still commemorated on that date to this day. Nine months after March 25 is December 25.

There is a popular theory that Christmas began to be celebrated in Rome at the same time as the pagan festivities for the winter solstice, locally considered to be December 25.

In AD 354, Philocalus wrote a text that dates the nativity of Jesus as December 25, and cites an earlier work as backup suggesting that Christmas was celebrated in Rome on the present date as early as AD 335.

The "official" choice of December 25 was probably made by Pope Julius I in the 4th century AD, almost certainly because this coincided with the pagan rituals of *Winter Solstice*, or *Return of the Sun*. The idea, which seems to have worked very well, was to replace the pagan celebration with the Christian one.

Over a period from 1582 to the late 18th century, initially only in Catholic countries, 11 days were dropped from the year when the switch from the Julian calendar to the Gregorian calendar was made. Some Christian church sects, called *old calendarists*, still celebrate Christmas on January 7 currently equivalent to December 25 in the Julian calendar.

Christmas failed to gain universal recognition as an important date, even among Christians, until relatively recently. In some protestant-dominated areas of USA, such as the Massachusetts Bay Colony, the celebration of Christmas was even legally banned, due to the community's refusal to accept the parts of the liturgical calendar which have no definite foundation in the scriptures. A few present day Christian churches, notably the Jehovah's Witnesses, some Puritan groups, and some ultra-conservative fundamentalist Christian denominations, still view Christmas as a pagan holiday not sanctioned by the Bible, and so do not celebrate it.

Until well into the 20th Century Christmas was not even a legal holiday in many places. This explains why nineteenth-century readers found it credible that Scrooge could require Bob Cratchit to come to work on Christmas Day (Dickens' *A Christmas Carol*) and why in the nineteenth century the US Congress could meet on Christmas Day.

ADVENT

The word *advent*, from Latin, means *"the coming"* and is the Christian celebration of Christ's first coming and anticipation of his return, or *second advent*. It is the start of the Christmas season and has been observed since the fourth century. It begins on the Sunday nearest November 30, (St Andrew's day), and extends to Christmas eve. Because the date on which it begins changes from year to year, so does the length of each advent season. In 2005 advent begins on November 27.

Originally advent was a time when converts to Christianity readied themselves for baptism. During the middle ages, advent became associated with preparation for the *second coming*. In early days it lasted from November 11, the feast of St. Martin, until Christmas Day and was considered a sort of pre-Christmas season of Lent when Christians devoted themselves to prayer and fasting.

The orthodox Eastern church observes a similar Lenten season, from November 15 until Christmas, rather than advent.

The tradition of *advent wreaths* originates in northern Europe, where in winter people lit candles on wheel-shaped bundles of evergreen. Both the evergreen and the circular shape symbolized ongoing life. By the 16th Century Eastern European Christians had adopted this practice and were making Advent wreaths much as we know them today.

An advent wreath traditionally contains four candles – originally three were purple and one rose (though nowadays white and red are as common). Purple dyes were once so rare and expensive that they were associated with royalty and the bishops. The three purple candles in the Advent wreath symbolize hope, peace, and love and are lit on the first, second, and fourth Sundays of Advent. The rose candle, which symbolizes joy, is usually lit on the third Sunday. Sometimes a fifth candle is placed inside the Advent wreath, to be lit on Christmas Day. It is white, the colour associated with angels and the birth of Jesus.

An *advent* calendar is a card or poster with twenty-four small doors, one to be opened each day from December 1 until Christmas Eve, each revealing a picture. This popular tradition started in Germany in the late 1800s and soon spread throughout Europe and then to USA. Many Advent calendars today have no religious content and are simply considered a fun way of counting down the days until Christmas. So now we have traditional Advent calendars depicting angels and biblical figures and others whose doors open to display teddy bears, pieces of chocolate, or photos of pop stars.

*"Christmas, children, is not a date.
It is a state of mind."*
Mary Ellen Chase

*"Christmas is the day that
holds all time together."*
Alexander Smith

THE TWELVE DAYS OF CHRISTMAS
————AND THE OTHER FEASTS————

On *Epiphany* (January 6), 12 days after December 25, the celebration of Christmas comes to an end and the decorations must be taken down and the tree removed from the house. To do so earlier is thought to bring bad luck for the rest of the year.

From the middle ages until the mid-nineteenth century Twelfth Night was more popular than Christmas day, and even today some countries celebrate Epiphany as the most important day of the Christmas season.

From the 5th century onwards there have been a number of traditional feasts following Christmas. The first three were December 26, the feast of St. Stephen – the day for giving leftovers to the poor (think of the carol "Good King Wenceslas"). St. John the Evangelist was commemorated on December 27; he was the only one of the twelve disciples who did not die a martyr. He said the famous words in the bible: "*The Word was made flesh, and dwelt among us*". On December 28 there is the feast of the Holy Innocents, to remember the children murdered by Herod.

On Epiphany the celebration of Christmas comes to an end. Epiphany celebrates the visit of the magi, the baptism of Jesus, and the turning of the water into wine. In the modern Western tradition, the activities of the three kings are the most important aspect, but in the Eastern church Jesus' baptism tends to be the primary theme.

In the Bucharest (Romania) subway on 6 January children leading lambs walk through the trains in commemoration of *the Lamb of God*. Orthodox Christians traditionally have their homes blessed with holy water on or around this day.

In the middle ages, the three feasts on December 26, 27 and 28 were each dedicated to a different part of the clergy. St Stephen was the patron of deacons, John the Evangelist of the priests, and the feast of the Holy Innocents was dedicated to young men training for the clergy. The subdeacons objected that they had no feast of their own so it became their custom to celebrate the "Feast of Fools" around January 1. The theme of "misbehaviour" recurs constantly at this time of year.

In the Netherlands, Germany, Scandinavia, and Poland, Christmas Day and the following day are sometimes called *First and Second Christmas Day*. In UK and many former Commonwealth countries, December 26 is referred to as Boxing Day, while in Ireland and Romania it is known as St. Stephen's Day.

The play *Twelfth Night* (as readers of Shakespeare know) is the ultimate celebration of Christmas madness. Shakespeare's play features one of his many "wise fools" who understand the real meaning of life better than those who think they are sane.

"Christmas begins about the first of December with an office party and ends when you finally realize what you spent, around April fifteenth of the next year."
P. J. O'Rourke

Winter Festivals & Traditions

November 1 – All Saints Day
November 11 – St. Martin's Day (Germany)
Last Thursday in November –
Thanksgiving Day (USA)

Fourth Sunday before Christmas –
Advent begins

December 6 – St. Nicholas Day
December 8 – The Immaculate Conception
December 10 – Hannukah begins (date varies)
December 13 – Santa Lucia's Day (Italy, Sweden)
December 15-16 – Posados or Novena begins
December 17 – Hannukah ends (date varies)
December 19. – St. Nicholas Day (Julian Calendar)
December 20 – St. Ignatious' Day in Romania
December 20-21 – Winter Solstice
December 21 – St. Thomas' Day
December 23 – Little Christmas in Denmark

December 24 – Christmas Eve
December 25 – Christmas Day
December 26 – St. Stephen's Day
Boxing Day in England

December 28 – Holy Innocents Day
December 30 – Bringing in the Boar

December 31 – New Year's Eve,
St. Sylvester's Eve, Hogmanay in Scotland

January 1 – New Year's Day, St. Basil's Day

January 2 – Snow Day, Holde's Day
January 3 – Evergreen Day
January 4 – St. Distaff's Day
January 5 – Epiphany Eve
January 6 – Epiphany, Three Kings Day
Twelfth Night
January 7 – Russian Orthodox Christmas
First Monday after Epiphany –
Plough Monday in England
January 13 – Twentieth Day
St. Knut's Day in Scandanavia

"In the old days, it was not called the Holiday Season; the Christians called it 'Christmas' and went to church; the Jews called it 'Hanukka' and went to synagogue; the atheists went to parties and drank. People passing each other on the street would say 'Merry Christmas!' or 'Happy Hanukka!' or (to the atheists) 'Look out for the wall!'"
Dave Barry

A *Lord of Misrule* was often chosen at Christmas to organise the festivities until Epiphany. This is one of the lost characters of the medieval Christmas celebration. It was customary around mid-November for peasants throughout Europe to draw lots for the title and the lord wore a crown of paper and multi-coloured clothes and was generally free to misbehave and encourage everyone else to do so. The paper hats in Christmas crackers may well hark back to this tradition.

A schoolboy was traditionally chosen as a *Boy Bishop* on December 6 (the Feast of St. Nicholas, renowned for his compassion for children) and he filled all the functions of the bishop (except for celebrating mass) until Holy Innocents' Day (December 28).

The Christmas season also sometimes saw the *Feast of the Ass* commemorating the donkey in the manger. On this day people were supposed to bray like a donkey at the points in the Mass where they would normally say "Amen."

The medieval church frowned on most of these practices, and the Reformers in the 16th century finally suppressed them.

THE PAGAN BACKGROUND

The Romans celebrated *Saturnalia* in honour of Saturn, god of agriculture, in late December and later specifically on December 21, the winter solstice in the northern hemisphere. They believed that the shortest day of the year was the birthday of the sun. The Roman emperor Constantine was a member of the sun-cult before converting to Christianity in 312 AD. At this festival gifts were exchanged, schools and courts were closed, war was outlawed, and slaves and masters ate at the same table, a tradition followed by the British army to this day, with officers serving junior ranks in the mess on Christmas day.

It may well be that the early Christians chose to celebrate Christ's birth on December 25 to make it easier to convert the pagan tribes. Referring to Jesus as the *light of the world* also fit with existing pagan beliefs about the birth of the sun.

The *yule log* tradition comes from Northern Europe and, particularly, Scandinavia. The dark, cold winters naturally resulted in the evolution of traditions concerned with warmth and light. Yuletide, meaning *the turning of the sun* or the

winter solstice, has traditionally been a time of great impor-
tance in many countries, but especially Scandinavia, with its
long, dark winter months.

The yule log was originally a whole tree, brought into the
house with great ceremony and celebration. The lower end
would be placed in the fireplace while the rest of the tree
stuck out into the room. The tree would be slowly fed into
the fire over a period of days. In some cultures it must be lit
from a piece of the previous year's tree.

There is an old English custom of bringing in the *Yule
Boar*. This consists of the head of a boar, nowadays more
commonly a pig, paraded on a silver platter on Christmas Day.
The Boar represents the spirit of abundance and prosperity,
of fertility and wealth. Fierce, strong and dangerous, it had
a special place in the heart of a warrior. Its ritual sacrifice at
the darkest time of the year would guarantee bountiful crops
in the next harvest, victory in battle and the vanquishing
of the old enemy - the long, dark nights of winter. There is a

very similar Scandinavian tradition involving the sacrifice of
the *sonartoltr* or *atonement boar.*

Wassail comes from the Old Norse *ves heill* — *be of good health.*
This evolved into the tradition of visiting neighbors on
Christmas Eve and drinking to their health.

WASSAIL CUP
(serves 6-8, depending how much each one drinks…)

Ingredients:
One bottle inexpensive red wine, cloves, 1 orange,
mulling spices. (ginger, cinnamon, nutmeg, mace)

Insert the cloves into the orange, point inward.
Cover orange fairly fully leaving about 1 cm / ½ inch
between each clove. Fill paper coffee filter with mulling
spices. Staple the edges together to form a pouch of
mulling spices. Pour wine into a pan. Be careful, red
wine stains even ceramic. Put the pan on a low or
medium heat. Place clove-stuffed orange and mulling
spice pouch in wine. Let it get hot, stirring all the
while. Don't let it boil or cook for too long as alchohol
evaporates at a lower temperature than water. Serve in
heat tolerant cups/mugs.

(In Germany this is called *Glühwein*, in Scandinavia,
Gløgg — sometimes with a dash of vodka or rum or
brandy added at the end …)

THE MISCHIEF-MAKERS OF
CHRISTMAS

St Nicholas is always accompanied by a mischievous companion
whose job tends to be the
punishing of badly-behaved
children. In Germany he was
known as *Knecht Ruprecht* (also,
in different parts of the country
as *Knecht Nikolaus, Nickel,
Pelznickel, Pelzmantel, Hans Muff,
Hans Trab* or *Klaubauf*). In Austria
and most of Eastern Europe he is
called *Krampus* and has horns and
is covered in bells and chains. He

carries a stick to beat the children and dresses in furs.
Sometimes he carries a sack on his back to take away
the naughty children.

The French equivalent is *Pére Fouettard* (the whipper) and
the Swiss have *schmutzli*, literally *the dirty little man*. Both
of them carried out the same kind of child-punishing
function, though nowadays it is obviously toned down.
Black Peter (*svarte Piet*) is the Dutch companion of the
saint, though he is a more modern invention and is
mischievous in a friendly rather than a threatening way.

A witch is an ongoing feature of Christmas celebrations,
particularly in Italy, where she is known as *la befana*, a
corruption of the Greek *epiphania*, (modern *Epiphany*). The

roots of this legend lie in Norse and Germanic myth. Jacob Grimm wrote of the travelling goddess named *Berchta* or *Holla*. *Frau Holle* is one of the names used in Germany for the wife of *Wotan* or *Odin*, and her Nordic name is *Frigg* or *Freya*. *Holla* is the mother of the Gods and lives deep in the mountains in a cave. She has the power to regenerate the sun after the darkness of the northern winter.

Befana is the witch who has become associated with the Epiphany and she would leave gifts in the stockings and shoes of well behaved children and coal for those who had misbehaved. Hearths were swept clean for her inspection, doors and windows decorated with evergreens, holly and mistletoe; refreshments were left out for her and cakes were baked that could be hollowed out and filled by her with gifts.

In Bavaria, Germany, there still lingers the custom of three disguised women known as *Berchten* moving in procession through the village on the Feast of the Epiphany. In Norse legend a Yule log burned on an altar of flat stone made for *Berchta*, keeping back the darkness and offering the hope that the sun would return again. *Berchta* is the root word for the tree we call *birch*.

The Greeks had the legend of the *Kallikantzaroi*, ugly mischievous sprites who roamed around during the long nights around the Winter Solstice performing malicious practical jokes. Old shoes were burned so that the smell would drive them off.

CUSTOMS & TRADITIONS

CHRISTMAS TREES

Christmas trees are an ancient tradition, though in England they only became popular after Queen Victoria's husband Albert, who came from Germany, made a tree part of the celebrations at Windsor Castle in the mid 1800's. They are known to have been popular in Germany as far back as the sixteenth century where the first printed reference to Christmas trees appeared in 1531.

When St. Boniface was preaching among the German tribes, he is said to have cut down an oak tree that was sacred to the Germans. As the tree fell it crushed all the other trees around it except a fir-tree. This fir, Boniface declared, was the tree of Christ and this is why it became associated with Christmas in Germany.

An early mention of a Christmas tree is found in legal documents from the city of Riga in Latvia. In 1510 it is stated that members of a local merchant guild carried a fir-tree decorated with artificial roses to the marketplace. They danced around it and then set it on fire.

For *Saturnalia* the Romans decorated their trees with suns, candles and small pieces of metal and today we still bring trees into our homes and hang decorations on them.

Since ancient times, evergreen trees have been a symbol of sexual potency and fertility, and played an important role in winter celebrations. In Norse legend *Yggdrasil* was the *Great Tree of Life*. In Northern Europe the evergreen was a reminder that winter would end and the green of spring would return.

In the United States, the earliest known mention of a Christmas tree is in the diary of a German who settled in Pennsylvania in the 18th Century.

Every year since 1947 the city of Oslo has presented to the British a spruce tree as a token of appreciation for their support during the Second World War. It stands in Trafalgar Square and is the most famous Christmas tree in Britain.

The best selling Christmas trees are Scotch pine, Douglas fir, Noble fir, Fraser fir, Virginia pine, Balsam fir and white pine. According to the *National Christmas Tree Association*, Americans buy over 37 million real Christmas trees each year. California, Oregon, Michigan, Washington, Wisconsin, Pennsylvania and North Carolina are the top Christmas tree producing states. Oregon is the leading producer of Christmas trees – cutting or uprooting some 9 million each year.

CHRISTMAS DECORATIONS

Originally, European Christmas tree decorations were candles, or home-made paper flowers, or apples, biscuits, and sweets. The earliest commercial decorations came from Nuremburg in Germany, a city famous for the manufacture of toys.

One German legend has it that late one night Martin Luther, the father of protestantism was walking in the woods and so enjoyed the sight of the stars twinkling through the branches of the trees that he cut down a small evergreen and brought it home, recreating the stars by placing candles upon the tree's branches.

Three years after Thomas Edison invented the electric light bulb in 1879, Edward H. Johnson, who worked for Edison's company, designed some light bulbs specifically intended for Christmas trees. He proudly displayed his electric tree lights at his home on Fifth

Avenue, New York City. They caused a sensation although some years were to pass before mass-manufactured Christmas tree lights were widely available.

In 1880, F.W. Woolworth went to the town of Lauscha in Germany, famous for its glass ornaments and bought a few as Christmas tree ornaments. Within a day he had sold out so the next year he bought more and within a week they, too, had sold. The year after that he bought 200,000 Lauscha ornaments. During the First World War supplies of ornaments from Lauscha ceased, so American manufacturers began to make their own, developing new techniques that allowed them to turn out as many ornaments in a minute as could be made in a whole day in Lauscha.

"Never worry about the size of your Christmas tree. In the eyes of children, they are all 30 feet tall."
Larry Wilde

"Remember, if Christmas isn't found in your heart, you won't find it under the tree"
Charlotte Carpenter

The modern Christmas custom of displaying a *wreath* on the front door comes from ancient Rome's New Year's celebrations. Romans wished each other "good health" by exchanging branches of evergreens. They called these gifts *strenae* after *Strenia*, the goddess of health. The custom was to bend these branches into a ring and display them on doorways.

The word *mistletoe* hs its roots in the old English word *mistel* which, like the modern German word *Mist*, means *dung*. It was originally thought to grow from birds' droppings on the branches of trees.

Mistletoe was considered to have magic powers by ancient Celtic and Teutonic peoples. It was known to heal wounds and increase fertility. The Celts hung mistletoe in their homes in order to bring themselves good luck and ward off evil spirits, gathering it at both the mid-summer and winter solstices. Using mistletoe to decorate houses at Christmas is a survival of this tradition.

Kissing under the mistletoe is first reported at the Graeco-Roman festival of *Saturnalia*. The mistletoe, and dung which they believed created it, were thought to enhance fertility.

In medieval times branches of mistletoe were placed over house and stable doors to prevent the entrance of witches, and hung from ceilings to protect the home from evil spirits. Farmers would give a bunch of mistletoe to the first cow that calved in the New Year to bring good luck to the herd.

Norwegian tradition has a gift-bearing little gnome or elf known as *Julebukk*, a goat-like creature harking back to Viking times when pagans worshipped Thor and his goat. During pagan celebrations a person dressed in a goatskin, carrying a goat head, would burst in upon the party and during the course of evening would "die" and return to life. During the Christian era, the goat began to take the form of the devil, and would appear during times of wild merry-making and jubilation. By the end of the Middle Ages, the game was forbidden by the Church and the state. In more recent times the goat has re-emerged in the tamer form of *Julebukk*.

Plum pudding, or *Christmas pudding*, has its origins in a Celtic legend of the harvest god *Dagda*, who made a stew out of all the good things of the Earth. Some centuries later, in England, the only thing that people were supposed to eat on Christmas eve was *frumenty*, a kind of corn-based porridge. Over the years the recipe has changed and eggs, fruit, spices, meat and dried plums were added. The whole mixture was wrapped in a cloth and boiled. Finally the meat was omitted and fruit, sugar and so on added to give us the sweet pudding eaten today.

Candy canes are hugely popular in USA but they come originally from Cologne, Germany. In around 1670 the choir-master of the Cathedral had the idea of handing out 'sugar sticks' to keep the children quiet during the Christmas Eve service. The sugar-sticks were bent to look like a shepherd's crook, also the symbol of the bishops. At that time the canes were of plain white sugar. Candy canes are first reported in USA in 1840 but appear to have got their familiar red stripes only in the 20th Century.

"Santa Claus wears a red suit, he must be a communist.
And a beard and long hair, must be a pacifist.
What's in that pipe that he's smoking?"
Arlo Guthrie

SANTA CLAUS

The name *Santa Claus* derives from St. Nicholas via the Dutch *Sinterklaas* and was first used in USA. Saint Nicholas Day (December 6) is still the traditional day for giving gifts to children in Holland. This Dutch custom was brought to America by the early settlers in New Amsterdam, which was renamed New York when the British took over the colony.

Saint Nicholas was the bishop of Myra in Lycia, which is in modern Turkey, some time before AD 350. The legends that have built up around his life associate him with acts of kindness to children. He was a widely admired saint throughout the eastern and western churches.

It is said that one day St Nicholas climbed the roof of a house and dropped a purse of money down the chimney. It landed in a stocking which a young girl had put to dry by the fire, hence the belief that Father Christmas comes down the chimney and places gifts in children's stockings.

All of Santa's American mail goes to Santa Claus, Indiana. There is also a town called Santa Claus in Arizona, a Noel in Missouri, and Christmases in both Arizona and Florida.

North American Aerospace Defense Command (NORAD) "tracks" Santa Claus' global transit each year, to wide attention by the mass media. Progress can be followed on NORAD's website www.noradsanta.org

Santa has to visit around 350 million children in some 100 million homes around all the world's time zones. This works out at about 880 visits per second.

Finnish people believe that Father Christmas (Santa Claus) lives in the northern part of Finland called Korvatunturi, north of the Arctic Circle. People from all over the world send letters to Santa Claus in Finland. (It is only fair to say that the people of Greenland say that Father Christmas actually lives in their country…)

In Iceland, people believe in thirteen Santas, known as *jólasveinar*. They begin visiting Icelandic homes on December 12th and, by Christmas Day, they've all arrived. Originally they were mischievous, each one making his presence felt in a different way; *Door Slammer* awakens sleepers by slamming doors, *Candle Beggar* snatches candles and *Meat Hooker* tries to run off with the meal. Nowadays they are quite benign and bring presents to the children.

Kris Kringle comes from the German *Christkindl* or Christ child. Dutch and German protestants who had settled in USA, especially Pennsylvania, anglicised the word and soon the original meaning was lost as today's Kris Kringle bears a greater resemblence to St Nicholas than to a holy child. Kris Kringle is still popular as the Santa Claus in various parts of the world today. He usually carries a small Christmas tree, entering the house through a window, decorating the tree and placing presents under it. He rings a bell to let the household know of his departure.

The other Pennsylvanian Santa-type character was *Belsnickle*, again from the German, *Pelz-Nikolaus*, which means "Nicholas in fur"

The actual gift givers at Christmas differ from country to country.

Brazil Father Christmas *Papai Noel*
Chile Old Man Christmas *Viejo Pasquero*
Colombia Baby Jesus *el niño Jesus*
England Father Christmas
France Father Christmas *Pere Noel*
Germany the Christ-child *Christkind*
Holland St Nicholas *Sinter Klaas*
Hungary Mekulash and Krampusz (on St Nicholas' day)
Italy a kindly old witch *La Befana*
Spain and much of **South America** The Three Kings
Russia In some parts - *Babouschka* (a grandmotherly figure) in other parts, Grandfather Frost.
Scandinavia a variety of Christmas gnomes, one is called *Julenisse*.
Syria Christmas-gifts are brought by a camel. The Three Wise Men made their journey to Bethlehem on camels. The smallest camel was exhausted by the long journey, but because he wanted to see the Christ child so much, Jesus blessed him with renewed strength and a long life so every year he brings gifts for the children

"Let me see if I've got this Santa business straight.
You say he wears a beard, has no discernible source of income
and flies to cities all over the world under cover of darkness?
You sure this guy isn't laundering illegal drug money?"
Tom Armstrong

"I played Santa Claus many times, and if you don't believe it,
check out the divorce settlements awarded my wives."
Groucho Marx

"I stopped believing in Santa Claus when I was six.
Mother took me to see him in a department store and
he asked for my autograph."
Shirley Temple Black

"I never believed in Santa Claus because I knew
no white man would be coming into my neighborhood
after dark."
Dick Gregory

"Santa Claus has the right idea. Visit people once a year."
Victor Borge

"Santa is even-tempered. Santa does not hit children
over the head who kick him. Santa uses the term folks rather
than Mommy and Daddy because of all the broken homes.
Santa does not have a three-martini lunch.
Santa does not borrow money from store employees.
Santa wears a good deodorant."
Jenny Zink
(To employees of Western Temporary Services, then the
world's largest supplier of Santa Clauses, quoted in
The NY Times 21 Nov 1984)

Our image of Father Christmas and what he gets up to is derived largely from a small number of literary sources.

————————

A Christmas Carol is the story of the ill-tempered and miserly Ebenezer Scrooge, who rejects compassion and philanthropy, and Christmas as a symbol of both, until he is visited by the *Ghosts of Christmas Past*, *Present* and *Future*, who show him the consequences of his ways. Dickens certainly had a great influence on the modern Christmas of English-speaking countries (tree, plum pudding, carols, etc.) and the movement to make Christmas day a public holiday.

Before settling on the name of Tiny Tim for his character in *A Christmas Carol*, three other alliterative names were considered by Charles Dickens. They were Little Larry, Puny Pete, and Small Sam.

Clement Clarke Moore's poem *A Visit from St. Nicholas*, popularly known as *The Night Before Christmas* (published in Sentinel, 1823) first described the rotund Santa and his sleigh landing on rooftops on Christmas Eve. He gave Santa 8 reindeer, all with

names, and had him coming down the chimney with his gifts. Two of the reindeer were called *Dunder* and *Blixem*, Most people are more familiar with the names from the 1940's song *Rudolph the Red Nosed Reindeer* where they are called Dasher, Dancer, Prancer, Vixen, Comet, Cupid, Donner and Blitzen.

American novelist Washington Irving (1783-1859) put him in his story, *A History of New York*, (by "Diedrich Knickerbocker") in 1809. This was a satire on New York's Dutch heritage including the legend of St Nicholas. Irving revised the book 3 years later adding details about Nicholas' "*riding over the tops of the trees, in that selfsame wagon wherein he brings his yearly presents to children.*" His Santa Claus was still known as St. Nicholas. He did smoke a pipe, and fly around in a wagon (without any reindeer), but he did not have his red suit or live at the North Pole

It was an American cartoon by Thomas Nast in Harper's Weekly on January 3, 1863 that first depicted Santa Claus with a sleigh and reindeer. He was delivering Christmas gifts to soldiers fighting in the U.S. Civil War. The cartoon was entitled "Santa Claus in Camp".

In 1881, the Swedish magazine *Ny Illustrerad Tidning* published Viktor Rydberg's poem *Tomten* featuring a painting by Jenny Nyström of the

traditional Swedish mythical character *tomte*, (an elf or goblin) which she turned into the white-bearded friendly figure now associated with Christmas. It was further developed in 1931 by Haddon Sundblom for the Coca-Cola Company and this image is very much what we expect the modern Santa to look like

But by 1927 (before the Coca Cola Santa's first appearance) The New York Times was able to report:

> *A standardized Santa Claus appears to New York children. Height, weight, stature are almost exactly standardized, as are the red garments, the hood and the white whiskers. The pack full of toys, ruddy cheeks and nose, bushy eyebrows and a jolly, paunchy effect are also inevitable parts of the requisite make-up.*

Not all traditional Christmas stories have Dickens' happy ending. *The Little Match Girl* of Hans Christian Andersen is a destitute little slum girl who walks barefoot through the cold and snow-covered streets on Christmas Eve, trying in vain to sell her matches, and looking in at the celebrations in the homes of the more fortunate. She dares not go home because her father is drunk. Unlike Ebeneezer Scrooge she meets a tragic end.

CHRISTMAS CARDS

The British Post Office expects to handle over 100 million cards EACH DAY, in the three weeks before Christmas.

The custom of sending Christmas greetings by post started in Britain in 1840 when the first 'Penny Post' public postal deliveries began. As printing methods improved, Christmas cards were produced in large numbers from about 1860. They became even more popular in Britain when a card could be posted in an unsealed envelope for one half-penny - half the price of an ordinary letter.

In America in 1822, the postmaster of Washington, D.C., complained he had to add 16 mail carriers at Christmas to deal with greeting cards alone. He wanted the number of cards a person could send limited by law.

In 1875 a German immigrant by the name of Louis Prang published the first line of U.S. Christmas Cards. Before this time cards were imported from Europe.

The first charity Christmas card was produced by UNICEF in 1949. The picture chosen for the card was painted by a seven-year-old girl, Jitka Samkova of Rudolfo, a small town in the former Czechoslovakia. The town received UNICEF assistance after World War II, inspiring Jitka to paint some children dancing around a maypole. She said her picture represented "joy going round and round."

EARLY CHRISTMAS CARDS

The first commercial Christmas card sold was designed by London artist John Calcott Horsley in 1843. He was hired by a wealthy British man, Henry Cole, to design a card that showed people feeding and clothing the poor on either side of a convivial picture of a Christmas party. The card's message was, "Merry Christmas and a Happy New Year to you." Of the original one thousand cards printed for Henry Cole, only twelve exist today. The printers at the time thought such cards were a passing fad and few originals were kept. They were sold at the time for one shilling (5p/9 cents) each. One of these cards, measuring 5 x 3 inches, hand-coloured by Horsley and sent by Sir Henry Cole to his grandmother in 1843 was sold at auction in England in 2001 for £20,000 ($37,000).

The "trick card" featuring some element of surprise became the most popular Christmas card of the Victorian era. While seeming straightforward at first glance, the turning of a page, the pulling of a string, or the moving of a lever or tab would reveal something unexpected.

There were pull-out flower cards and an example from 1870 shows red, white and yellow roses encased in a fan-shaped handle. Pull the silken thread dangling from the handle and the card opens to twice its original size and five separate roses come into view, each surrounded with lilies of the valley and accompanied by quotes from Wordsworth and Keats.

Another popular trick card used realistic reproductions of banknotes, realistic enough to be deceptive when the card was first opened. The "Bank of Love" card was so similar to a real five pound note that it was withdrawn soon after being issued. Cards resembling cheques would be issued from 'The Bank of Blessings" for "Ten Thousand Joys." Railway tickets were printed with "Prosperity" being the destination from "All Difficulties," transferable "Only To Old Friends."

The largest group of trick cards were "tab cards", consisting of two cardboard sections attached at the edges while a tab between the two enabled a different scene or text to be brought into view when pulled. One such card considered daring in the late 1880's wished the receiver a "Joyous Yuletide" but featured a young woman whose legs moved as if dancing when the tab was pulled.

ODDS & ENDS

Long ago in Scandinavia it was considered dangerous to sleep alone on Christmas Eve. The extended family, master and servant, alike would sleep together on a freshly spread bed of straw.

At lavish Christmas feasts in the middle ages, swans and peacocks were sometimes served *endored* or gilded, their flesh painted with saffron dissolved in melted butter, to look like gold. The birds were then served wrapped in their own skin and feathers, which had been removed and set aside prior to roasting.

The tradition of Christmas lights may date back to when Christians were persecuted for saying Mass. A simple candle in the window meant that Mass would be celebrated there that night.

Hot cockles was a popular game at Christmas in medieval times. It was a game in which the other players took turns striking the blindfolded player, who had to guess the name of the person delivering each blow. *Hot cockles* was still a Christmas pastime until the Victorian era.

In England, the *Holy Days and Fasting Days Act* of 1551, which has not yet been repealed, states that every citizen must attend a Christian church service on Christmas Day, and must not use any kind of vehicle to get to the service.

The Christmas turkey first appeared on English tables in the 16th century, but didn't immediately replace the traditional fare of goose, beef or boar's head in the rich households.

The eating of mince pies at Christmas dates back to the 16th century. Some still say that to eat a mince pie on each of the Twelve Days of Christmas will bring 12 happy months in the year to follow.

In 1647, the English parliament passed a law that made the celebration of Christmas illegal. Festivities were banned by the puritan leader, Oliver Cromwell, who considered feasting and revelry, on what was supposed to be a holy day, to be immoral. The ban was lifted only when the Puritans lost power and the monarchy was restored in 1660.

Jack Horner was a steward to the Abbot of Glastonbury, and he had to take a pie to King Henry VIII as a present from the Abbot. The pie contained title deeds to 12 manors sent to the King in the hope that he would not pull down Glastonbury Abbey. The King only received 11 deeds. Horner was of course suspected of stealing one.

Little Jack Horner
Sat in the corner,
Eating of Christmas pie:
He put in his thumb,
And pulled out a plum,
And said, "What a good boy am I!"

Tom Smith, a confectioner, invented Christmas crackers in 1850, as a way of selling more of his confections. They have never really caught on except in the UK.

Franklin Pierce 14th President of the United States (from 1853-1857) was the first to decorate an official White House Christmas tree

In Victorian England, turkeys were popular for Christmas dinners. Some of the birds were raised in Norfolk, and taken to market in London. To get them to London, the turkeys were supplied with boots made of sacking or leather. The turkeys were walked to market. The boots protected their feet from the frozen mud of the road.

"Dear Lord, I've been asked, nay commanded, to thank Thee for the Christmas turkey before us... a turkey which was no doubt a lively, intelligent bird... a social being... capable of actual affection... nuzzling its young with almost human-like compassion. Anyway, it's dead and we're gonna eat it. Please give our respects to its family." Berke Breathed

To raise money to pay for a charity Christmas dinner in 1891, a large crabpot was set down on a San Francisco street, becoming the first Salvation Army collection kettle or collecting box.

When Robert Louis Stevenson, author of *Treasure Island*, died on December 4, 1894, he willed his November 13 birthday to a friend who disliked her own Christmas birthday.

"Yes, Virginia, there is a Santa Claus. . . Thank God!
He lives, and he lives forever. A thousand years from now,
Virginia, nay ten times ten thousand years from now,
he will continue to make glad the heart of childhood."
Francis Pharcellus Church
"The Sun" Sept 21, 1897

The *Christmas club*, a savings account in which a person saves money regularly to be used at Christmas for shopping, came about in England around 1905.

*"Christmas is a race to see which gives out first -
your money or your feet."*
Anon

In 1914, at the first Christmas of World War I, German troops fighting in the Flanders trenches offered a truce to the British, French and Belgians on the other side. Against the express orders of some of the officers soldiers stopped shooting, exchanged gifts and even played a game of soccer in no-man's land.

Hallmark introduced its first Christmas cards in 1915, five years after the founding of the company.

The world's first singing radio-commercial was aired on Christmas Eve, 1926 in USA for the *Wheaties* cereal. The Wheaties Quartet, who sang the jingle, comprised an undertaker, a bailiff, a printer, and a businessman and they performed the song live for the next six years, at $6 per singer per week (£3.35). The commercials were a resounding success.

The biggest selling Christmas record ever, Bing Crosby's *White Christmas*, was released in 1942.

"To perceive Christmas through its wrapping becomes
more difficult with every year"
E. B. White

During World War II it was necessary for Americans to mail Christmas gifts early for the troops in Europe to receive them in time. Shops joined in the effort to remind the public to shop and mail early and the protracted shopping season and the expression "post early for Christmas" were born.

In the British armed forces it is traditional that officers wait on the men and serve them their Christmas dinner. This dates back to a military custom from the middle ages but may go right back to the traditions of "misrule" at the time of the winter solstice.

According to a recent survey, 7 out of 10 British dogs get Christmas gifts from their owners.

"I once bought my kids a set of batteries for Christmas with
a note on it saying, toys not included."
Bernard Manning

Christmas trees are edible, at least in part... The needles are a good source of vitamin C. Pine nuts, which are found in the pine cones, are also an excellent source of nutrition.

During the Christmas/Hanukkah season in USA, more than 1.75 billion candy canes will be made.

Formerly called Kiritimati, Christmas Island in the Indian Ocean is the world's largest coral atoll. It was discovered by Captain Cook on Christmas Eve 1777.

The best-selling Chritmas movie ever is *It's a Wonderful Life,* whose hero, George Bailey, is a businessman who sacrificed his dreams to help his community. On Christmas Eve, a guardian angel finds him in despair and prevents him from committing suicide, by magically showing him how much he means to the world around him.

New York City's Empire State Building's lights are turned off every night at midnight with the exception of New Year's Eve, New Year's Day, Christmas Eve, Christmas Day, and St. Patrick's Day, when they are illuminated until 3 a.m.

Queen Elizabeth's Christmas message to the nation was televised for the first time on December 25, 1957. The first British monarch to broadcast a Christmas message to his people was King George V who broadcast on BBC radio.

"A lovely thing about Christmas is that it's compulsory, like a thunderstorm, and we all go through it together. "
Garrison Keillor

"Christmas isn't a season. It's a feeling."
Edna Ferber

WHO WAS BORN ON CHRISTMAS DAY?

1642 - Sir Isaac Newton (mathematician)
1821 - Clara Barton (nurse: the founder of
         American Red Cross)
1876 - Mohammed Ali Jinnah (founder of the
         republic of Pakistan)
1887 - Conrad Hilton (hotel magnate)
1899 - Humphrey Bogart (actor)
1908 - Quentin Crisp (actor)
1914 - Tony Martin (Alvin Morris) (singer)
1915 - Pete Rugolo (bandleader, arranger:
         Stan Kenton)
1918 - Anwar el-Sadat (Egyptian president;
         Nobel Peace Prize winner)
1932 - Little Richard (Penniman) (singer):
1937 - O'Kelly Isley (singer; the Isley Brothers)
1945 -Noel Redding (bass player with
         Jimi Hendrix)
1946 - Jimmy Buffett (songwriter, singer)
1948 - Barbara Mandrell (singer)
1949 - Sissy (Mary) Spacek (actress)
1954 - Annie Lennox, (singer)
1958 - Ricky Henderson (baseball player)

The sign of the zodiac for those born on 25 December
is Capricorn.

QUOTES BY PEOPLE BORN ON 25 DECEMBER

"Things are never so bad they can't be made worse."
"People who don't drink are afraid of revealing themselves"
Humphrey Bogart

*"Never keep up with Joneses. Drag them down to your level.
It's cheaper."*

*"The war between the sexes is the only one in which both sides
regularly sleep with the enemy"*
Quentin Crisp

*"We either make ourselves miserable, or we make ourselves strong.
The amount of work is the same."*

*"All paths lead nowhere, so it is important to choose a path that
has heart"*

*"A man of knowledge lives by acting, not by thinking
about acting."*
Carlos Casteneda

*"Success seems to be connected with action. Successful people
keep moving. They make mistakes, but they don't quit."*
Conrad Hilton

*"If I have seen further than others, it is by standing
upon the shoulders of giants."*
Isaac Newton

WHO DIED ON CHRISTMAS DAY?

1921 – Hans Huber (composer)
1926 – Yoshihito 123rd Emperor of Japan
1930 – Harvey Worthington Loomis (composer)
1946 – WC Fields writer/comedian/actor
1954 – Johnny Ace (ballad singer, dies at 25 in a
      game of Russian Roulette)
1957 – Frederick Law Olmsted (US architect of
      Central Park)
1977 – Charlie Chaplin (actor)

1980 - Oscar Romero (archbishop of El Salvador, murdered)

1983 - Joan Miro (artist)

1985 - George Rhodes (orchestra leader, Sammy Davis Jr Show)

1989 - Nicolae Ceausescu (dictator of Romania, executed together with his wife, Elena)

1995 - Dean Martin (singer/actor)

1996 - Jon Benet Ramsey, (Colorado child beauty queen, murdered age 6)

1998 - Bryan MacLean, (Rock & Roll singer & guitarist, The Byrds)

WHAT HAPPENED ON DECEMBER 25TH?

0 – Jesus' birthday

336 – Christmas first celebrated in Rome.

800 – Charlemagne's coronation

1066 – William the Conqueror's coronation as King of England

1776 – General George Washington's forces cross the Delaware River to attack the British at Trenton, New Jersey.

1818 – The song *Silent Night* is performed for the first time at the church in Oberndorf, Austria.

1926 – Hirohito becomes Emperor of Japan.

1932 – An earthquake in Gansu, China kills 70,000 people

1939 – *A Christmas Carol* is read on US radio for the first time.

1941 – The British military garrison in Hong Kong surrenders to Japan.

1950 – Walt Disney first broadcast on US TV, with a one-hour Christmas special

1975 – Cyclone Tracy hits Darwin, Australia

1991 – Russian president Gorbacev resigns

QUOTATIONS

TRADITIONAL AND SENTIMENTAL
"The best Christmas of all is the presence of a happy family
all wrapped up with one another."
Anon

"Christmas gift suggestions: To your enemy, forgiveness.
To an opponent, tolerance. To a friend, your heart.
To a customer, service. To all, charity. To every child,
a good example. To yourself, respect."
Oren Arnold

"The only real blind person at Christmas-time is he who has
not Christmas in his heart."
Helen Keller

CYNICAL
"In the United States Christmas has become the rape of
an idea."
Richard Bach

"Next to a circus there ain't nothing that packs up and
tears out faster than the Christmas spirit."
Kin Hubbard

"Christmas to a child is the first terrible proof that to travel
hopefully is better than to arrive"
Stephen Fry

"Bloody Christmas, here again,
Let us raise a loving cup,
Peace on earth, goodwill to men,
And make them do the washing up"
Wendy Cope

"Why is Christmas just like a day at the office? You do all the work and the fat guy with the suit gets all the credit"
Anon

"That's the true spirit of Christmas; people being helped by people other than me"
Jerry Seinfeld

"One of the nice things about Christmas is that you can make people forget the past with a present"
Anon

"From a commercial point of view, if Christmas did not exist it would be necessary to invent it."
Katherine Whitehorn

WITTY AND THOUGHTFUL

"Happy, happy Christmas, that can win us back to the delusions of our childhood days, recall to the old man the pleasures of his youth, and transport the traveler back to his own fireside and quiet home!"
Charles Dickens

"When we were children we were grateful to those who filled our stockings at Christmas time. Why are we not grateful to God for filling our stockings with legs?"
G. K. Chesterton

" What I don't like about office Christmas parties is looking for a job the next day."
Phyllis Diller

"Christmas is a holiday that persecutes the lonely, the frayed, and the rejected"
Jimmy Cannon

SONGS
AND VERSE

"On Christmas day you can't get sore,
Your fellow man you must adore,
There's time to cheat him all the more
The other three hundred and sixty-four"
Tom Lehrer

St Francis of Assisi was one of the earliest writers of secular Christmas songs. Written in the early 13th Century in Latin his words conveyed a Christian message but celebrated the joys and pleasures of Christmas as well, and with much less solemnity than was traditional.

The word *carol* comes from the Greek *choros* which was a dance, rather than a song. As dancing and the singing of anything other than hymns was frowned upon or even forbidden by much of the early church, carol singing was sustained as a secular, peasant tradition and only became widely popular in UK and USA after the publication of Dickens' *A Christmas Carol* in 1843. Most of the carols we sing today were written after that date.

Christmas carol-singing began as an old English custom called *wassailing* – which also involved drinking the health of one's neighbours in what today would be called *mulled wine*. The custom of singing carols is very old – the earliest English collection was published in 1521

God rest you merry, gentlemen,
   Let nothing you dismay,
For Jesus Christ, our Saviour,
   Was born upon this day,
To save us all from Satan's power
   When we were gone astray.
O tidings of comfort and joy!
   For Jesus Christ, our Saviour,
Was born on Christmas Day.
         Dinah Maria Mulock Craik

Christmas is here:
Winds whistle shrill,
   Icy and chill.
Little care we;
Little we fear
Weather without,
Sheltered about
The Mahogany Tree.
William Makepeace Thackeray
   "The Mahogany Tree"

Silent Night was first sung in 1818, in the village church of Oberndorf in Austria. Josef Mohr, an Austrian, and assistant priest at the church, had written the text in 1816. On

Christmas Eve, he went into the church and found that the organ was not working so he showed the organist, Franz Xaver Gruber the hymn he had written. Gruber composed a tune for it that could be played on a guitar – *Silent Night*. Mohr and Gruber sang the song in Church that evening, in two-part harmony. There are said to be over 300 versions of the hymn around the world today

The original first verse is:

Stille Nacht! Heil'ge Nacht!
Alles schläft; einsam wacht
Nur das traute heilige Paar.
Holder Knab' im lockigten Haar,
Schlafe in himmlischer Ruh!
Schlafe in himmlischer Ruh!

The popular Christmas song *Jingle Bells* was composed in 1857 by James Pierpont, and was originally called "*One-Horse Open Sleigh.*"

I heard the bells, on Christmas Day,
Their old, familiar carols play,
And wild and sweet
The words repeat
Of peace on earth, good will to men.
Henry Wadsworth Longfellow "Christmas Bells"

Love came down at Christmas,
Love all lovely, Love Divine;
Love was born at Christmas;
Star and angels gave the sign.
Christina Rossetti

There is a relatively recent and probably spurious theory that *The Twelve Days of Christmas* was used to help catholic children in England remember different articles of faith during the persecution by protestant monarchs. The "true love" represented God, and the gifts all different ideas:

The **"Partridge in a pear tree"** was Christ.

2 Turtle Doves – The Old and New Testaments

3 French Hens – Faith, Hope and Charity – the Theological Virtues

4 Calling Birds – the Four Gospels and/or the Four Evangelists

5 Gold Rings – The first Five Books of the Old Testament, the "Pentateuch", which tells the story of man's fall from grace.

6 Geese A-laying – the six days of Creation

7 Swans A-swimming – the seven gifts of the Holy Spirit, the seven sacraments

8 Maids A-milking – the eight beatitudes

9 Ladies Dancing – the nine Fruits of the Holy Spirit

10 Lords A-leaping – the ten commandments

11 Pipers Piping – the eleven faithful apostles

12 Drummers Drumming – the twelve points of doctrine in the Apostle's Creed

There is no real evidence for this entertaining theory. The origins of the song, whose earliest known appearance in print is in the 1780 children's book *Mirth Without Mischief*, are not known. Perhaps it began as a Twelfth Night game in which one person recited a verse, which everyone else repeated; he then added a second verse and so on until someone made a mistake and had to pay a penalty or forfeit. There are French versions of the song, and the partridge, for example, was first introduced to England from France in the 1770s, suggesting a French origin for the song.

Rudolph the Red-Nosed Reindeer was created in 1939 as a marketing tool for the US stores group Montgomery Ward. An employee, Robert L May, was asked to come up with a short story that could be given away in booklet form to customers over the holiday season. By 1946 over 6 million copies had been distributed. May's brother Johnny Marks wrote the song in 1947 and in 1949 it was recorded by the singing cowboy, Gene Autrey, and sold 2 million copies in its first year, going on to become the second best-selling Christmas record after *White Christmas*.

The time draws near the birth of Christ;
The moon is hid; the night is still;
The Christmas bells from hill to hill
Answer each other in the mist.
Alfred, Lord Tennyson "In Memoriam"

At Christmas I no more desire a rose
Than wish a snow in May's new-fangled mirth;
But like of each thing that in season grows.
William Shakespeare "Love's Labour's Lost"

'Twas Christmas broach'd the mightiest ale;
'Twas Christmas told the merriest tale;
A Christmas gambol oft could cheer
The poor man's heart through half the year.
Sir Walter Scott "Marmion"

CHRISTMAS AROUND THE WORLD

(Clearly this section will contain a lot of generalisations as traditions vary from one part of a country to another and from one family to another - and nowadays the pace of change is fast. The "snapshots" of different cultures are meant to be no more than that!)

"May you have the gladness of Christmas
which is hope;
The spirit of Christmas which is peace;
The heart of Christmas which is love."
Ada V. Hendricks

Gift giving in **Argentina** occurs on January 6, or *Three Kings Day*, when children leave shoes under their beds to be filled with snacks or small gifts by the Magi, who stop off on their way to Bethlehem. Nativity scenes are a feature of Christmas, both in homes and in public places, here and all over South America. In regions with large numbers of Native American descendants the figures are often hand-carved in a centuries-old style. As in Mexico, village processions acting out the events surrounding the birth of Christ are also common. Christmas lights are seen everywhere, and with the summery weather, firework displays are common.

In **Armenia** the traditional Christmas Eve meal consists of fried fish, lettuce, and spinach. The meal is usually eaten after the Christmas Eve service

In **Austria** & **Germany** Christmas celebrations start with the feast of St Nicholas on December 6. The saint accompanied by the devil (Krampus) asks children for a list of their good and bad deeds. Good children are given sweets, toys and nuts. During Advent many homes will have an *Adventskranz* (Advent wreath). On each Sunday of Advent, another candle is lit. Children leave letters on their windowsills for the *Christkind*, decorated with glue and sprinkled with sugar to make them sparkle. Germans and Austrians bake beautiful gingerbread houses and cookies and you can buy these at the Christmas markets to be found in the town squares all over both countries during the month of December.

The German Christmas tree pastry, *Christbaumgebäck*, is baked in all sorts of shapes for tree decorations. On December 24 the tree is decorated, a family meal enjoyed, traditionally featuring carp or goose, and presents are exchanged. The Christkind brings presents and decorates the Christmas tree for the children who must wait until they hear a bell tinkling. Then they enter the room where the tree is waiting, often decorated with real candles.

RECIPE FOR GERMAN GINGERBREAD
*for gingerbread boys or girls, hearts, or
Hansel-and-Gretel houses.*

2 ½ tablespoons of golden syrup
150g (½ cup) of butter
100 g (½ cup) of brown sugar
egg yolk
400g (2 cups) of plain flour
level teaspoon of bicarbonate of soda,
    free of lumps
3 level teaspoons of ground ginger
dash of cinnamon, optional
extra flour for rolling pastry
currants, peel, cherries and a little icing

Stand container of golden syrup in hot water to soften.
Beat the butter and sugar to a cream, then beat the egg
yolk. Beat in the syrup. Slowly add flour, bicarbonate of
soda, ginger and an optional dash of cinnamon. With
floury hands knead into a dough. Wrap in a plastic bag or
shrink-wrap and place in fridge for 1 hour. Brush flour on
the rolling pin and under the dough. Roll to an even 10
mm (⅓ inch) thick and cut out whatever shapes you
choose. Place on a greased tray about 2 cms (¾ inch) apart
and bake in a moderately slow oven (180°C / 350°F) for
about 12 minutes. Leave for a few minutes and remove
with a spatula. Decorate with icing, peel, cherries etc.

In 1937, the first postage stamp to commemorate Christmas
was issued in Austria. The next year Adolf Hitler replaced
Santa.

Christmas in **Australia** is based on the British tradition but while the northern hemisphere is in the middle of winter, Australians are baking in temperatures as high as the mid 30 degrees (95°F). It is no surprise then that some Australians have their Christmas dinner at midday on the beach and Bondi Beach in Sydney can attract thousands of people on Christmas Day, though restrictions on the consumption of alcohol in public, introduced in 2004, may change this. The traditional Australian Christmas dinner is turkey, ham, or pork with plum pudding for dessert. A small good-luck token will often be baked inside the pudding, a relic of the English tradition of putting small silver coins (three-penny pieces) in the pudding. It is, not surprisingly, becoming more and more common to have a Christmas meal which suits the weather rather better, such as a seafood salad. The major cities all organise public open-air carol-concerts in the weeks leading up to Christmas.

In **Belarus** Christmas is celebrated twice: on December 25 and on January 7 because the country has both Catholic (15%-20%) and Orthodox (65%-70%) believers. Both dates are official holidays.

On the sixth of December *Sinterklaas* (*Saint-Nicholas*) is celebrated in **Belgium** and although it marks the beginning of the Christmas season it is an entirely different holiday from Christmas. St. Nicholas pays two visits to each house. On December 4 he comes to find out how each child has behaved. On the evening of December 6 (the feast day of St. Nicholas), he returns to leave presents for those who have been good. Father Christmas is called *de Kerstman* in the Flemish-speaking northern part of the country, and *le Père Noël* in French-speaking south. He comes around on

Christmas day to bring presents for the children. Presents are exchanged within the family too, and are placed under the tree, or put in stockings near the fireplace, to be found on the morning of December 25. Christmas breakfast is a sweet bread called *cougnou* or *cougnolle* – the shape is supposed to represent the baby Jesus. Most families will have another big meal on Christmas day. In rural areas particularly the three kings go through the village singing carols on January 6.

In **Brazil** Father Christmas is called *Papai Noel.* Many Christmas customs are similar to USA or UK. For those who have enough money, a special Christmas meal will be chicken, turkey, ham, rice, salad, pork, fresh and dried fruits, often with beer. Poorer people will just have chicken and rice. The Brazilians love a firework display at this time of year.

In **Britain** *Father Christmas*, wearing a long red robe, flies on a sleigh drawn by reindeer and comes down the chimney bringing presents which he leaves in stockings late on Christmas Eve, after the children have gone to sleep. The gifts are usually opened the following day. Children used to send letters to Father Christmas by burning them up in the fireplace. It was thought that the requests were carried to Father Christmas in the smoke. On Christmas Eve it is traditional to leave a carrot out for the reindeer and mince pies, brandy or a glass of milk for Father Christmas.

In **England** the traditional Christmas dinner, usually eaten at lunch time. or in the early afternoon, is roast turkey, or, less commonly, goose, with fried pork sausages, roast potatoes, sprouts and cranberry sauce. For dessert it is Christmas pudding. Mince pies, pastry cases filled with a mixture of chopped dried fruit, are also enjoyed by most households. Most families will pull Christmas crackers when they sit down to eat; these contain small gifts, jokes and paper hats. The festival of Nine Lessons and Carols at King's College, Cambridge is a popular religious programme and features annually on radio and TV.

CHRISTMAS PUDDING

The Christmas pudding originated as a porridge in the middle ages. It was made of beef, mutton, raisins, currants, prunes, wine, and mixed spices. Known as *frumenty*, it was eaten as a fasting dish before the Christmas celebrations began. In the 16th century, it became known as plum pudding. The meat was left out and dried fruit and brandy were added along with eggs to thicken it. It was banned by the Puritans in the 1600's, but was reintroduced by George I in 1714 after he had tried it and thought it was delicious. It became universally popular in Victorian times.

There are thousands of individual recipes for plum pudding. It is a British Christmas tradition that a wish made while mixing the Christmas pudding will come true only if the ingredients are stirred in a clockwise direction.

The day after Christmas Day, December 26 is known as *Boxing Day*. This derives from the custom which started in the Middle Ages when churches would open their alms boxes (boxes in which people had placed gifts of money) on the day after Christmas and distribute the contents to the poor. The tradition continues today as gifts of money are often given to delivery workers such as postmen, the milkman and the children who deliver newspapers; this gift is known as *a Christmas box*. Boxing Day is celebrated in Great Britain and in most areas settled by the English (the U.S. is the major exception), including Canada, Australia, and New Zealand. If Christmas falls on a Friday or a weekend there is a Boxing Day public holiday on the following Monday.

RECIPE FOR SCOTTISH BANNOCKS
Traditional Christmas meal.

150g (2 cups) oatmeal
200g (1 cup) flour
1 teaspoon salt
225g (¾ cup) butter or margarine
½ cup boiling water

Mix dry ingredients together in a bowl. Add the butter cut with a knife into small pieces and mix with the fingertips until the mixture resembles coarse bread-crumbs. Add the water to the mixture. Mix to a dough. Roll out until quite thin and then cut into rounds about 10cm/4in diameter. Cook in a pre-heated hot oven for 10-12 minutes.

Some people believe that Christmas is downplayed in **Scotland** because of the influence of the Presbyterian

Church (or Kirk), which considered Christmas a "Papist," or Catholic event. As a result, Christmas in Scotland tends to be relatively understated whereas New Year's eve, or *hogmanay*, is a major celebration.

In **Bulgaria** under communism Santa Claus was known only as *Grandfather Frost*. Now he is again also called *Father Nicholas.* He goes from house to house and fills large bags with presents. *Koledni gevreci*, round buns, and *bansia*, pastries, are eaten at Christmas and on December 24 a meal of 7, 9, or 11 courses is prepared. The house is decorated with hay to remind the family of the manger.

Canada follows much the same basic traditions as USA (see below), with regional differences influenced by the nationalities of the original settlers. In **Labrador**, children get hollowed-out turnips with a lighted candle inside. In **Nova Scotia**, during the twelve days of Christmas small groups of masked mummers, *belsnicklers*, go around the neighborhood ringing bells, making noise, and demanding treats. Children may be quizzed by the mummers on their behaviour and be rewarded with sweets and candy if they say they have been good, much in the same way as the European St Nikolaus / Krampus tradition. In **Quebec**, where the language and tradition is predominantly French, they display *crèches* (cribs) in their homes and after attending midnight mass, families may be served *tourtiere* (pork pie) or *boulettes* (small meatballs). The Christmas meal is called a *reveillon* and Xmas goes on until the *fete du roi* (party of the king) on January 6.

One fairly new, unifying tradition started in 1986 but has caught on: public parks and buildings across Canada are lit for the holidays at the same moment, 6:55 on the first Thursday in December.

The Christian children of **China** decorate trees with paper ornaments in the shapes of flowers, chains and lanterns. and hang up stockings hoping for gifts and treats from *the Old Man of Christmas*. Chinese Christmas trees are called *Trees of Light*. Christians are a small minority in China, which is officially atheist (the traditional religion contains elements of Confucianism, Taoism, and Buddhism). For most Chinese, the major winter celebration and extended public holiday is the New Year, or *Spring Festival*, which occurs in January or February and is celebrated with special meals and taking time to pay respect to the ancestors. Children receive gifts of new clothes and toys and families celebrate with firework displays.

In the **Czech Republic**, Christmas is celebrated mainly on December 24, or Christmas Eve, or "open-handed day", when the gifts are given in the evening. December 25 and 26 are also holidays. Gifts are brought by *little Jesus*. Traditions include fasting on Christmas Eve until a ceremonial dinner is served. The gifts are displayed under the Christmas tree, usually spruce or pine, and people open them after dinner on the 24th. Other Czech Christmas traditions involve predictions. Apples are cut crosswise; if a star appears in the core, the next year will be successful, while a cross suggests a bad year. Girls throw shoes over their shoulders; if the toe points to the door, the girl will get married. Another tradition involves pouring molten lead into water and guessing a message from the shapes that appear when it hardens.

In **Ethiopia** the main celebrations take place at Epiphany and pilgrims from all over the country converge on the ancient city of Aksum, where they bathe in a large reservoir whose waters have been blessed by a priest.

In **France** Christmas is called *Noël*. This is derived from the French phrase *les bonnes nouvelles*, which means literally *the good news* and refers to the gospels. Most families have a Christmas tree, sometimes decorated in the traditional way with red ribbons and real white wax candles. Fir trees in the garden are often decorated too, with lights on all night. Father Christmas is called *Père Noël*. He visits on Christmas eve and is accompanied by his helper *Père Fouettard* whose duty is to tell *Père Noël* how each child has behaved during the past year. The Christmas meal is an important family gathering with good meat and the best wine. Christmas cards are not as popular as in many parts of the world and not everyone sends them. The traditional Christmas meals differ in the various regions of France. In southern France, for instance, a Christmas loaf (*pain calendeau*) is cut crosswise and is eaten only after the first part has been given to a poor person. In Brittany, buckwheat cakes and sour cream is a popular main dish. In Alsace, a roasted goose is the preferred main course but in Burgundy, turkey and chestnuts are preferred. In the Paris region, oysters are a hugely popular holiday dish, followed by a cake shaped like a Yule log.

Breton 'sonneurs'

RECIPE FOR FRENCH YULE LOG (*bûche de noël*)
Traditional Christmas Cake

> 475 ml (2 cups) heavy cream
> 60g (½ cup) icing (confectioner's) sugar
> 50g (½ cup) unsweetened cocoa powder
> 1 teaspoon vanilla extract
> 6 egg yolks
> 100g (½ cup) white sugar
> 30g (⅓ cup) unsweetened cocoa powder
> 1½ teaspoons vanilla extract
> ⅛ teaspoon salt
> 6 egg whites
> 50g (¼ cup) white sugar
> icing (confectioner's) sugar for dusting

Preheat oven to 190°C/375°F. Line a baking tray of approx 25 x 38cm (10 x 15 in) with greaseproof (parchment) paper. In a large bowl, whip cream, the icing (confectioner's) sugar and 50g (½ cup) of cocoa, and 1 teaspoon vanilla until thick and stiff. Refrigerate. In a large bowl, beat egg yolks with 100g (½ cup) sugar until thick and pale. Blend in 30g (⅓ cup) cocoa, 1½ teaspoons vanilla, and salt. In a large glass bowl whip egg whites to soft peaks. Gradually add 50g (¼ cup) sugar, and beat until whites form stiff peaks. Immediately fold the yolk mixture into the whites. Spread the batter evenly into the prepared pan. Bake for 12 to 15 minutes in the preheated oven, or until the cake springs back when lightly touched. Dust a clean dishtowel with the icing sugar. Run a knife around the edge of the pan, and turn the warm cake out onto the towel. Remove and discard greaseproof (parchment) paper. Starting at the short edge of the cake, roll the cake up with the towel. Cool for 30 minutes. Unroll the cake, spread the filling to within 1 inch of the edge. Roll the cake up with the filling inside. Place seam side down onto a serving plate, and refrigerate until serving. Dust with icing sugar before serving.

Greeks do not use Christmas trees or give presents at Christmas. A priest may throw a small cross into the village water to drive the *kallikantzaroi* (mischievous spirits) away. To keep them from hiding in dark, dusty corners, he has to go from house to house sprinkling holy water. There is a feast for St Basil's day (December 30) and after the meal the family lift the table three times for good luck.

Recipe for Kourabiethes
Greek shortbread

400g (2 cups) (flour
1 teaspoon vanilla
1 tablespoon ouzo (or a drop or two of
    aniseed essence and a dash of vodka)
450g (1½ cups) unsalted butter
2 egg yolks
175g (⅞ cup) sugar
2 teaspoons cinnamon
1 teaspoon baking powder
1 large handfull (½ cup) ground almonds
    or walnuts
icing (confectioner's) sugar and cloves

Sift flour with baking powder twice. Cream butter and sugar, add ouzo, vanilla and egg yolks, nuts, and cinnamon. Blend in flour to make soft but firm dough. If not enough liquid, add another egg yolk. Break off small pieces, pat into biscuit shape, place on floured baking tray. Insert a clove in each biscuit and bake at 180°C/ 350°F gas mark 4) for 20 mins (cooked but not brown). While still hot, sprinkle biscuits with icing (confectioner's) sugar. Each shortbread should be stuck with one clove to represent the three wise men who brought spices to the Christ child.

In **Holland** St Nicholas, *Sinter Klaas*, visits the homes of the children accompanied by *svarte Piet* or *Black Peter*, who carries a birch rod to punish those children who have been bad in the past year. Good children receive small gifts from the Saint but then get to play hunt-the-presents around the house for more substantial gifts. Christmas day celebrations are much more popular in Holland than they used to be.

The **Hungarian** Santa, called *Mekulash*, visits children on December 6th, St. Nicholas' Day, and children put boots in the windows for gifts. Well-behaved children get tangerines, walnuts, apples, dates, chocolate wrapped in red paper and chocolate Mekulash figurines. Mekulash is usually accompanied by one or two small evil helpers, *krampusz*. If the child has been bad, the boot will contain just a stick usually with a devil figure attached, indicating that a beating is in order. The Christmas tree is decorated on Christmas Eve, never before, and the presents are placed under it. Most families decorate the tree together, but some families keep the older tradition that the tree should be a surprise for children, who are told it was brought by the angels. After dinner the tree is lit and the gifts are exchanged. Children enter the room only when bells ring to signify the visit of the angels.

In **Iceland** celebrations begin a day earlier than in many countries, on December 23, St. Thorlakur's day, named for Iceland's most important native saint. The main traditional food on this day is a simple meal of skate. The Yule tree is usually decorated on this evening and last minute gifts can be bought, with stores remaining open until midnight.

Jól or Yule celebrations start in Iceland at 6 p.m. on Christmas Eve, a custom going back to the times when the new day officially began at 6 p.m. So in Iceland there are thirteen rather than twelve days of Christmas. On December 24 TV transmission stops in Iceland around 5 p.m. and only restarts at 10 p.m. Traditionally the family listens to Evensong on the radio then has the evening meal after which presents are opened. It is generally the immediate family that spends Christmas Eve together. Traditional food includes *Hangikjöt* (smoked mutton) or *Rjúpa* (ptarmigan), which was once a poor man's dinner but has now become something of a luxury. Another specialty is *Laufabrau*, a leaf bread made of dough in very thin sheets cut into intricate patterns and fried (the Welsh *lavabread*, made with seaweed, is from the same linguistic root).

In **India** Christmas is now a holiday in most states but the Christmas season is celebrated actively in only a few parts of the country such as Mumbai (Bombay) and Goa but other states are catching up with Christmas celebrations in a bid to attract tourists. Christmas is known as *bada din* (the big day) in Hindi, and revolves around Santa Claus and shopping.

In **Ireland** lighted red candles decorated with sprigs of holly are placed in windows on Christmas Eve (December 24), to guide Joseph and Mary to shelter. Irish women used to bake a seed cake for each person in the house and make three puddings, one for each of Christmas Day, New Year's Day and Twelfth Night and after the evening meal on the 25th bread and milk were left outside the door as a sign of hospitality. Being Ireland, a bottle of Guinness (rather than the English glass of sherry) is left out for Santa with the mince pies.

The 26th December, St Stephen's Day, is also important, with hunting and other traditional sporting activities. In Ireland, unlike Britain, fox-hunting has not been made illegal.

Located in the West Bank area of **Israel**, Bethlehem is a popular destination for tourists and pilgrims. In the 4th century A.D., the emperor Constantine built the Church of the Nativity above the cave that is said to be the manger where Jesus was born. At Christmas-time the church is the scene of numerous processions and observances. Christian homes often have a cross painted over the house door and many will display a home-made manger scene.

La Befana, a kindly witch, rides a broomstick down the chimney to deliver toys into the stockings of **Italian** children. Legend has it that Befana was sweeping her floors when the three wise men stopped and asked her to come to see the baby Jesus. She replied that she was too busy. Later, she changed her mind but it was too late. So, to this day, she goes

---

RECIPE FOR AMARETTI
Traditionally served at Christmas time in Italy.

2 egg whites
¼ teaspoon salt
100g (½ cup) sugar
1 cup chopped blanched almonds
¾ teaspoon almond extract

Add salt to egg whites and beat until frothy. Add sugar   gradually, beating until mixture is stiff but not dry. Add almonds and almond extract and fold in gently. Drop almond mixture on buttered and floured baking sheet by the teaspoon, shape into small mounds, leaving room between each mound. Let stand 2 hours. Bake at 190°C / 400°F/gas mark 6) for 12 minutes or until they are delicately brown in colour.

out on Christmas Eve searching for the baby and leaving gifts for the "holy child" in each household. In recent years *Babbo Natal*, a Santa Claus-like figure, is becoming more common.

In **Japan** only 1 per cent of the population are Christian but most Japanese enjoy giving each other gifts and like to decorate their homes with evergreens during Christmas. There is no tradition of a big Christmas meal; it is a time when people try to think of and help the less fortunate members of society.

In **Latvia** the Christmas celebration is know as *Ziemassvetki* or winter festival, a direct descendent of ancient winter solstice celebrations. A central element to *Ziemassvetki* is the log burning which involves groups of people dragging a log around the house during the day, burning the log all night singing songs and drinking beer. Latvians believe that *Father Christmas*, a stern looking man dressed in gray, with a long white beard, brings presents on each of the 12 days of Christmas starting on Christmas Eve. Usually the presents are put under the family Christmas tree. The Latvian Christmas Day meal is lentils or peas with bacon, meat pies, cabbage and sausage.

In **Luxembourg** the presents are given on December 6, St. Nicholas Day. If the children have been good, St. Nicholas comes the night before and leaves gifts. If there is a knock on the door, that means the children have been bad and the *Husicker* or *Black Peter* is coming. He carries a big basket full of twigs, sticks and coal. If the children have been really bad Black Peter may chain them to his belt and carry them off kicking, screaming and crying through the village so that every one will know which children have misbehaved.

From **Mexico** comes the tradition of the *posada* which celebrates the Holy Family's journey to Bethlehem. It can be traced back to St. Ignatius Loyola who, in the 16th century suggested that special prayers (a *novena*) be said on nine successive days at Christmas. A religious pageant developed out of this and was introduced to the natives in Mexico by Spanish missionaries at the end of the century. Gradually these solemn and deeply religious observances turned into more of a fun event and, eventually, started being celebrated in people's homes and the community, rather than in the church.

The *posada* today begins with a procession that sets off as soon as it gets dark with a child dressed as an angel leading the procession, followed by two more children carrying figures of Mary and Joseph on a litter covered with with twigs and straw. Groups of children carrying flowers follow and after them come the grown-ups and the musicians. When the procession reaches the house chosen for that evening, it divides into two groups, one representing the holy pilgrims, the other the innkeepers.

The angel and the children bearing the figures of the Holy Family file through the house followed by the pilgrims until they arrive at a closed door, behind which are the

innkeepers. The pilgrims knock on the door asking for a room. There is then a series of exchanges between the travelers asking for shelter and the innkeepers refusing until they finally relent and welcome the exhausted strangers: "Enter, holy pilgrims. Come into our simple home and into our hearts. This is a happy time for here beneath our roof we can offer shelter to the Mother of God."

Everyone then enters and kneels to pray, after which the fun begins with fireworks, sweets called *colaciones*, and plenty to eat and drink. These ceremonies go on for eight nights but on the ninth evening, Christmas Eve, a particularly impressive *posada* takes place, during which an image of the infant Jesus is carried in by two people who have been selected as the godparents and this image is placed in a crib or manger. The people in the procession carry *faroles*, transparent paper lanterns containing lighted candles, on long poles and sometimes a Christmas Eve posada will have people representing the Holy Family, with Mary riding a real donkey.

Traditionally Advent is an important season in **Poland** with daily early-morning church services, known as *Rororaty*. On Christmas Eve, melted beeswax is poured into water, and fortunes are divined from the shapes which emerge. There is a similar traditiion in much of central Europe using molten lead on New Year's Eve. There are beautifully-lit Christmas trees in every town outside churches and in homes. The trees are traditionally decorated with natural produce such as apples, walnuts, chocolate and candles. On the top of the tree is a star or a straw angel.

As in much of Europe, December 24 is the key date for family celebrations. A traditional Christmas food is *Oplatek* which is a decorative bread signifying the body of Christ, and which used to be carried from house to house to wish people a Merry Christmas. Nowadays, the bread is still shared with members of the family and immediate neighbours. As each person eats the bread he must forgive any wrongs done to him over the year and wish the perpetrators good luck. An ancient tradition during the Advent period is the display of cribs in the square of Krakow's Walwel cathedral. Artists from all over Poland create crèches or cribs known as *Szotka*, These range in size from a few inches to several feet in height and they remain on display until Christmas Eve. The best of them are then displayed in the museum.

The **Philippines** has a long Christmas season starting on 16 December with the first of the 9 daily dawn-masses, also known as *gift-masses*. Like other countries influenced by hispanic culture, the nativity scene is highly visible and lamp posts are decorated with Christmas lanterns. Christmas Eve is is known as *noche buena* and the traditional Christmas feast is eaten after midnight mass. Family members dine together on *queso de bola* (cheese) and *jamon* (Christmas ham). On Christmas Day children visit their godparents who give them gifts and wish them a prosperous and joyful life.

In **Portugal** Father Christmas brings presents to children on Christmas Eve. The presents are left under the Christmas tree or in shoes by the fireplace. A special Christmas meal of salted dried cod with boiled potatoes is eaten at midnight on December 24.

In **Russia**, under the communists, many Christian traditions were suppressed and the religious festival of Christmas was substantially replaced by the *Festival of Winter*. Russians did manage to keep some traditions alive by shifting them to New Year's Day, including the visit by gift-giving *Grandfather Frost* and his *Snowmaiden*. Many current customs, including their Christmas tree, or *yolka* were brought by Peter the Great after his western travels in the late 18th century. Old traditions, however, die hard and although there are few today who will say prayers and fast for 39 days, there are many who will celebrate Christmas Eve, which for the othodox Christians of Russia is January 6. The Russian Orthodox church uses the old *Julian* calendar for religious celebration days. When the first evening star appears in the sky they begin a huge supper of twelve courses, which celebrate each of the twelve apostles - fish, beet soup (*Borsch*), stuffed cabbage, stuffed goose, dried fruit and lots more. On Christmas Day, January 7, hymns and carols are sung in churches which have been decorated with the usual Christmas trees, flowers and red and green lights. *Babushka* (meaning *grandmother*) is the traditional Christmas figure who gives the presents to the children. It is said that she refused to accompany the three wise men to see Jesus because of the cold weather but then regretted not going and so set off to try and catch up, filling her basket with presents. She never found Jesus so now goes from house to house, leaving toys for well-behaved children.

In **Scandinavia** candles represent an important part of Christmas and every home is filled with them. Indeed the traditional celebration of *Santa Lucia* on December 13 is extremely important, especially in **Sweden**. The young girls wear an evergreen wreath with seven lighted candles on their head and a white robe with a red sash and take breakfast in bed to the rest of the family. St. Lucia, whose name means "light", was a Christian martyr who died in the 4th century A.D. and her feast day originally marked the winter solstice.

RECIPE FOR SWEDISH NUTS

150g (1 cup) whole almonds
150g (½ cup) butter or margarine
2 egg whites,1 cup sugar, dash salt
2 handfulls (1 cup) each of pecan and
     walnut halves

Spread almonds on a baking tray (cookie sheet) and bake at 175°C / 325°F / gas mark 4) until lightly browned, about 15-20 minutes, stirring occasionally; cool. Melt butter in a 35 x 25 x 5 cm (13 x 9 x 2 inch) baking pan. Beat egg whites until foamy; add sugar and salt, and continue beating until stiff. Fold in all of the nuts; spread mixture in baking pan over melted butter. Bake at 175°C / 325°F / gas mark 4) for about 30 minutes or until mixture is browned and all the butter is absorbed, stirring and turning every 10 minutes to cook evenly.

The tradition of Yule Logs comes from this cold, northerly region. *Yule* (or *jul*) is the Scandinavian word for *Christmas*. It is said that the presents are brought by gnomes who live in the attics of houses all the year round, known as *Julebukk* or *Julenisse*. Nisse guards all the farm animals and plays tricks on the children if they forget to place a treat out for him. Medieval laws in **Sweden** declared a Christmas peace (*julefrid*) for twenty days starting on Christmas day, during which fines for robbery and manslaughter were doubled. Swedish children still celebrate a party, throwing out the Christmas tree (*jul-gransplundring*), on the 20th day of Christmas, January 13, (*Knut's day*). A favourite Christmas meal in **Norway** is cod with boiled potatoes washed down with beer and punch. The **Danes** like to eat goose, duck, pork, red cabbage and potatoes and for dessert, rice pudding, whereas the traditional Swede goes for herring, ham and beans.

RECIPE FOR JULEGROED
This is served as part of a Danish Christmas meal.

600ml (3 cups) of milk
good teaspoon of butter
cup of washed white rice
75ml (⅓ cup) of double (thick) cream
a handful of almonds (according to taste)
50g (¼ cup) of sugar
a pinch of cinnamon powder

Using a large saucepan, heat milk until boiling. Add butter, then rice and turn down the heat. Cover and let the rice simmer very slowly and gently for an hour, or until all the milk is absorbed (check from time to time) and the rice is swollen up. When cooked, place in bowl and fold the cream and the almonds. Serve in small bowls sprinkled with sugar and cinnamon.

In **Finland** on Christmas Eve people eat rice porridge and plum juice in the morning and then decorate a spruce tree in the home. At mid-day, the *peace of Christmas* is broadcast on radio and TV from the city of Turku by its mayor, a ceremony which has been performed for some 700 years (not on the radio…). In the evening, a traditional Christmas dinner is eaten including casseroles containing macaroni, swede (rutabaga), carrot and potato, with ham or turkey. Many families will visit cemeteries and graveyards to place a candle onto the graves of family members. Children receive their presents on Christmas Eve. Many Finnish families hang a straw wreath on the front door and it is not taken down until Twelfth Night. For centuries, straw was the most important material for Finnish Christmas decorations.

One **Norwegian** Christmas custom begins in late autumn at harvest time. The finest wheat is gathered and saved until Christmas. This wheat is then attached to poles made from tree branches, making perches for the birds. A large circle of snow is cleared away beneath each perch. According to the Norwegians, this provides a place for the birds to dance, which allows them to work up their appetites between meals. Just before sunset on Christmas Eve, the head of the household checks on the wheat in the yard. If a lot of sparrows are seen dining, it is suppose to indicate a good year for growing crops.

Christmas is a summer holiday in **South Africa** and the traditions there are a mixture of English, Dutch and, to a lesser degree, African. As in England pantomimes such as "Babes in the Wood", founded on one of the oldest ballads in the English language, are very popular. Boxing Day on December 26 is observed as a holiday, another clear legacy of the British colonial past.

An artificial spider and web are often included in the decorations on **Ukrainian** Christmas trees. A web found on Christmas morning is believed to bring good luck. Christmas Day in the Ukraine can be celebrated on either December 25, according to the Gregorian calendar, or on January 7, which is the Orthodox or Julian calendar. A traditional sweet Christmas bread called *kolach* is placed in the middle of the dining table. This bread is braided into a ring, and three such rings are placed one on top of the other, with a candle in the center of the top one. The three rings symbolize the Holy Trinity. The table for Christmas Eve dinner in the Ukraine is set with two tablecloths, one for the ancestors of the family, the other for the living members. In pagan times, ancestors were believed to be benevolent spirits who, when shown respect, brought good fortune.

The **USA** is such a large country, with so many diverse immigrant traditions that it is difficult to generalise. The first Christmas observance in what is now the United States was celebrated in Spanish style by Hernando de Soto and his army, who set up their winter camp in the present day city of Tallahassee, Florida in 1539. Since that time, the holiday traditions of nearly every nation on earth have moved into, around, and across the U.S. The predominant Christmas traditions are still European and most Americans celebrate Christmas with the exchange of gifts and with family visits and with homes and trees decorated with glass balls, paperchains, tinsel and so on. Houses will be decorated inside with wreaths of holly and with mistletoe, and Christmas cards are displayed. Some homes are decorated outside with coloured lights and figures of reindeer or Santa Claus. For some the day begins on Christmas Eve with the Midnight Mass, with Christmas Day itself celebrated generally on December 25, except in communities with strong Nordic, German or East

European influence, where December 24 is the more important day. Dinner is usually roast turkey, goose, duck or ham served with cranberry sauce, then plum pudding or pumpkin pie followed by nuts and fruit. The other major US holiday, *Thanksgiving*, is celebrated at the end of November and the "holiday season" now lasts from mid-November until the end of the year, with Christmas carols on the radio and playing in shops for several weeks. It is deemed "politically correct" by many Americans today to wish people "happy holidays" rather than make any reference to Christmas.

The oldest city in USA is **St. Augustine**, **Florida**, where the entire historic area is hung just with white lights. There is a city ordinance which prevents anyone from displaying out-door Christmas lights that are not white, the exception being the Christmas tree in the town square that is set up under the white light-hung ancient oak trees.

In **Arizona** and **Texas**, the Mexican tradition known as *Las Posadas* is kept up with processions and a play representing the search of Mary and Joseph for a room at the inn. *Posada* means inn, or lodging, in Spanish. Families playing the parts visit each other's houses enacting and re-enacting the drama and, at the same time, having a look at each other's Christmas decorations, particularly the crib. In Fredericksburg, in the northern part of Texas you will find a German-style *Christmas Market*.

In **Hawaii**, Christmas starts with the coming of the Christmas Tree Ship bringing food and Santa Claus.

The South has a long Christmas tradition going back to the first English Christmas at Jamestown. Today in **New Orleans**, thousands of carolers gather each year in Jackson Square for a huge community sing-song and an ox, its horns decorated with holly and ribbons, is paraded through the streets, while bonfires are lit all along the Mississippi River.

In **Philadelphia** a street-procession called a mummers' parade lasts almost a whole day with bands, dancers and fancy dress.

In **New York City** well-known sights include the ice-skating rink beneath the tree at Rockefeller Center and the magnificent Neapolitan baroque figures on the *Angel Tree* at the Metropolitan Museum of Art.

In **Chicago's** Museum of Science and Industry, an enchanted forest of trees from around the world is created and displayed together with three cribs (crèches) decorated by community groups from different ethnic and cultural backgrounds. Appropriate ethnic food is served in the cafeteria and various folk dances and story hours take place throughout the season. Much of this can be seen on their website www.msichicago.org

In **Washington**, DC, the focal point of the season is the lighting of the tree on the Ellipse. A large tree represents the nation with smaller trees representing each state, while the Kennedy Center presents a wide-variety of Christmas events, a really popular one being the performance of Handel's *Messiah* at the concert hall.

Boston is also famous for its annual Christmas presentation of *The Messiah* by the Handel-Haydn Society as well as the carol-singing on Beacon Hill.

The *Nation's Christmas Tree* in **California's** Kings Canyon National Park is the site of an annual celebration. Carol-singers gather at the base of the 267-foot sequoia, the size of the group depending on the depth of the heavy snows in the park.

In Balboa Park, **San Diego**, California there is an annual Christmas concert on the world's largest outdoor pipe organ.

In **Bethlehem**, **Pennsylvania**, founded by Moravian missionaries on Christmas Eve, 1741 there is a huge *Christmas Market*. The decorations in most buildings in the city consist of a single candle in the window but a giant lighted star on the top of South Mountain can be seen from over twenty miles away.

In **Alaska**, children carry lanterns and long poles with a star on top from door to door. They sing carols and are invited in for a treat.

In parts of **New Mexico**, candles are lit in paper bags weighted down with with sand and placed on streets and rooftops to light the way for the Christ Child.

Alabama became the first state, in 1836, to declare Christmas a legal holiday. In 1907, **Oklahoma** became the last US state to do so.

MERRY CHRISTMAS! IN DIFFERENT LANGUAGES
(some of these also say Happy New Year!)

Merry Christmas, Nearly Everybody!
Ogden Nash

Albania – Gezuar Krishtlindjet
Argentina – Feliz Navidad y un prospero ano
nuevo
Azerbaijan (Azeri) – Tezze Iliniz Yahsi Olsun
Basque – Eguberri Zoriontsuak eta urte berri on
Belgium (Flemish) – Zalig Kerstfeest
Brazil (Potuguese) – Feliz Natal
Bulgaria – Vessela Koleda - Chestita Koleda -
Tchestito Rojdestvo Hristovo
Colombia – Feliz Navidad para todos
Croatia – Sretan Bozic
Cuba – Feliz Navidad
Czech Republic – Vesele Vanoce
Denmark – Glaedelig Jul
Esperanto – Gajan Kristnaskon
Estonia – Roomsaid Joulupuhi ja head uut aastat
Finland – Hauskaa Joulua
Fiji – Merry Christmas
France – Joyeux Noel
Germany and Austria – Frohe Weihnachten!
Fröhliche Weihnachten!
Greece – Eftihismena Christougenna
Hawaii – Mele Kalikimaka
Hungary – Boldog Karácsonyt - Kellemes
Karacsonyt es boldog uj evet
Iceland – Gledileg jol og farsaelt komandi ar-
Gledileg jol og Nyar

Indonesia – Salamet Hari Natal

Ireland – Nollaig Shona dhuit - Nodlaig mhaith
     chugnat

Israel – Mo'adim Lesimkha

Italy – Buon Natale e felice Capodanno -
     Buone Feste Natalizie

Jamaica – Merry Christmas

Japan – Merii Kurisumasu

Kazakhstan – Hristos Razdajetsja -
     Rozdjestvom Hristovim

Korea – Sung Tan Chuk Ha - Chuk Sung Tan

Latvia – Priecigus ziemas svetkus un Laimigu
     Jauno Gadu.

Lebanon – Milad Majeed

Liechtenstein – Fröhliche Weihnachten

Lithuania – Laimingu Kaledu - Linksmu Kaledu

Luxembourg – Schéi Krëschtdeeg a vill Glëck
     am Neie Joër!

Malaysia – Selamat Hari Krimas

Mexico – Feliz Navidad

Moldova – Craciun fericit si un An Nou fericit!

Mozambique – Boas Festas

Namibia – Geseende Kersfees

Netherlands – Prettige Kerstdagen - Vrolijk Kerstfeest
     en een Gelukkig Nieuwjaar - Prettig Kerstfeest

Norway – Gledelig Jul - God Jul og godt nytt aar

Pakistan – Bara Din Mubarrak Ho

Panama – Feliz Navidad

Papua – New Guinea Bikpela hamamas blong
     dispela Krismas

Peru – Feliz Navidad

Philippines – Maligayang Pasko

Poland – Wesolych Swiat Bozego Narodzenia

Portugal – Boas Festas
Romania – Sarbatori vesele - Craciun Fericit
Russia – Hristos Razdajetsja -Rozdjestvom
     Hristovim
Samoa – Ia Manuia le Kerisimasi
Saudi Arabia – Mboni Chrismen
Serbia – Srečan Bozic - Srečna Nova Godina
Slovakia – Vesele Vianoce
Slovenia – Srecen Bozic
Solomon Islands – Merry Christmas
South Africa (Afrikaans) – Gesëende Kersfees
Spain Feliz Navidad – (Catalan) Bon Nadal i
     Feliç Any Nou
Sri Lanka – Subha nath thalak Vewa - Nathar Puthu
     Varuda Valthukkal - Subha Aluth Awrudhak Vewa.
Sweden – God Jul och gott nytt År!
Switzerland – (Swiss-German) Fröhlichi Wiehnacht
     (French) Joyeux Noel
Thailand – Ewadee Pe-e Mai
Turkey – Noeliniz ve yeni yiliniz kutlu olsun
Ukraine – Srozhdestvom Kristovym - Veselykh
     Svyat i scaslivoho novoho roku
Uganda – Webale Krismasi
United Kingdom – Merry Christmas, Happy
     Christmas, (Wales) Nadolig Llawen, (Gaelic-Scots)
     Nollaig Chridheil agus Bliadhna Mhath Ur
United States – Happy Holidays
Viet Nam – Chuc mung Giang Sinh

"Blessed is the season which engages the whole world
in a conspiracy of love."
Hamilton Wright Mabi

ACKNOWLEDGEMENTS

As you may imagine, there are facts, figures and opinions about Christmas and particularly the different ways people celebrate the holiday, in many places. I used all kinds of sources and where opinions differed had to make a choice. I am quite happy to be corrected by my readers and can be contacted at info@ffnf.co.uk

The following sources were particularly helpful:

http://www.factmonster.com
www.wikipedia.com
en.thinkexist.com
http://www.santas.net/aroundtheworld.htm
http://www.christmas.com/worldview/
http://www.soon.org.uk/christmas.htm
http://www.corsinet.com/braincandy/xmastrivia.html
http://allrecipes.com/
http://www.snopes.com/holidays/christmas
http://www.newadvent.org
www.christmas-treasures.com

www.stcharleschristmas.com

"I hear that in many places something has happened to Christmas; that it is changing from a time of merriment and carefree gaiety to a holiday which is filled with tedium; that many people dread the day and the obligation to give Christmas presents is a nightmare to weary, bored souls; that the children of enlightened parents no longer believe in Santa Claus; that all in all, the effort to be happy and have pleasure makes many honest hearts grow dark with despair instead of beaming with good will and cheerfulness".
Julia Peterkin "A Plantation Christmas" (1934)